SURVIVING
a Tsunami

Nicolas Brasch

Rigby

www.Rigby.com
1-800-531-5015

Rigby Focus Forward

This Edition © 2009 Rigby, a Harcourt Education Imprint

Published in 2007 by Nelson Australia Pty Ltd ACN: 058 280 149
A Cengage Learning company

1 2 3 4 5 6 7 8 374 14 13 12 11 10 09 08 07
Printed and bound in China

Surviving a Tsunami
ISBN-13   978-1-4190-3709-2
ISBN-10   1-4190-3709-9

Acknowledgments
Illustrations by Melissa Webb
The author and publisher would like to acknowledge permission to reproduce material
from the following sources:
Photographs by AAP Image/ AFP, cover, pp. 1, 9, 11, 12 / EPA, p. 10; Fairfax Photos/
Jason South, p. 15 top; Lonely Planet Images/ Jerry Alexander, p. 4; Newspix/ AFP, p. 13;
Photolibrary.com/Pacific Stock, p. 5 top/ Photonica, p. 8/ Robert Harding Picture Library
Ltd, p. 15.

SURVIVING a Tsunami

Nicolas Brasch

Contents

WHAT IS A TSUNAMI?

In December 2004,
I was 12 years old and lived in **Indonesia**.
I went to school and helped my family.
Life was good.

Then on December 26, 2004, a tsunami hit many places
in Indonesia.

Indonesia

Before December 2004, I didn't know what a tsunami was.
Now I know all about them.
I even know how to say the word *tsunami*.
It sounds like *soo-NAH-mee*.

Some people think that a tsunami
is a giant wave, but a tsunami isn't just one wave.
A tsunami is a number of giant waves
that are set off by an **earthquake**.

The earthquake that started the tsunami in 2004 happened close to the coastline of Indonesia.

Let me tell you more...

shockwaves

earthquake epicenter

RUN FOR THE HILLS

Most days, I walked along the beach
to look for wood.
Wood is good for starting a fire.

On the day the tsunami hit,
I was walking along the beach
when I saw something very odd.
The **tide** was going out
when it should have been coming in.

I raced home to tell my family.

As I ran, I heard shouting close behind me.
I stopped and turned around.
People were shouting and looking at the sea.

A giant wave hit the beach
and raced over the land.
Houses and stores were washed away.

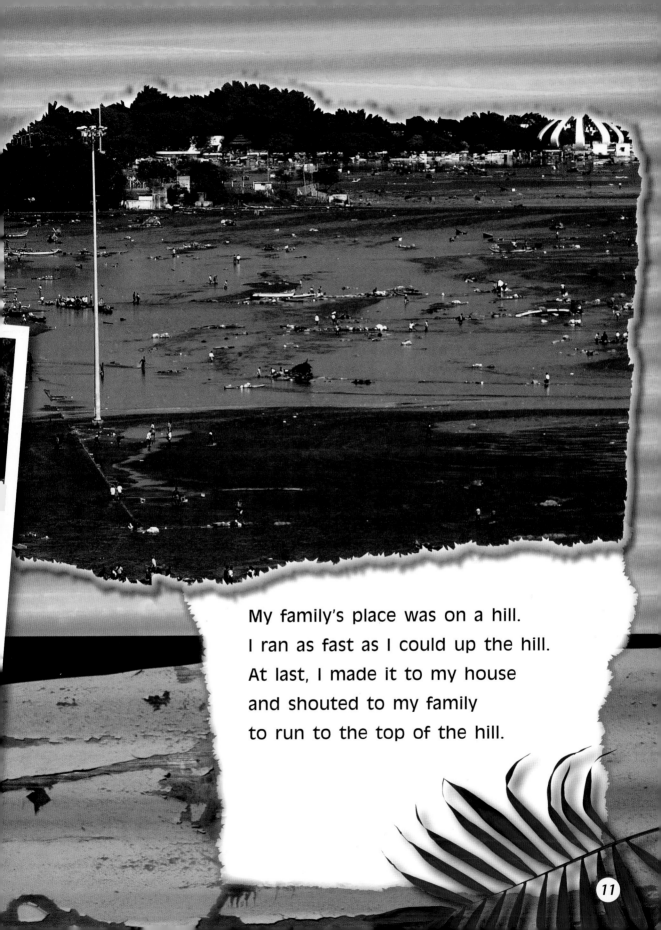

My family's place was on a hill.
I ran as fast as I could up the hill.
At last, I made it to my house
and shouted to my family
to run to the top of the hill.

A DISASTER FOR THE WORLD

We made it to the top of the hill.
From there, we saw the danger below.

Wave after wave crashed onto the beach
and raced over the land.
Many people couldn't run as fast as the waves
and were washed away with the houses and stores.

Later I found out that the tsunami didn't just hit Indonesia.

The tsunami hit countries all over Asia and as far away as Africa.

ASIA

Bangladesh

India

Thailand

AFRICA

Somalia

Myanmar

Kenya

Maldives

Malaysia

Sri Lanka

Tanzania

Indonesia

Madagascar

countries hit by the tsunami

I hope I never see a tsunami again.
But if I do, I will know what to do.
I will tell everyone
to run to the top of a hill.

Glossary

earthquake   a violent shaking of the ground

Indonesia   a country in Asia

tide   the regular rising and falling of the sea

Index